At Joe's Garden

At Joe's Garden

HARVEST RECIPES

from the PACIFIC NORTHWEST

Mary Ellen Carter

Photographs by Diane Padys

Printed in the United States of America.

Photography by Diane Padys, all photos ©L'Image Magick, Inc.
Prop Styling by Cynthia Verner
Design by Deborah Brown, View Design Company
Copy Editing by Carolyn Hyatt

Library of Congress Cataloging-in-Publication Data
At Joe's Garden: Harvest Recipes From The Pacific Northwest /
Mary Ellen Carter
ISBN# 0-9669514-2   At Joe's Garden etc.

Published by Joe's Garden
3100 Taylor Avenue
Bellingham, WA 98226

Table of Contents

A Brief History of Joe's Garden   9

Introduction   11

FIRST HARVEST   12

LEAFY GREENS   13

LETTUCES

Spicy romaine Lettuce with Avocado and Lime   13

Dilled Mushroom and Mixed Lettuce Salad   14

SPINACH

Spinach with Sautéed Shallots and Goat Cheese   15

Spinach Salad with Sesame Seeds   16

Fennel, Orange and Spinach Salad   17

CHARD

Linguine with Swiss Chard and Walnuts   18

Braised Swiss Chard   19

Italian Rice and Chard Soup   19

Wild and Weedy Greens   20

BEET GREENS

Sautéed Beet Greens with Garlic   21

ROOTS   22

RADISHES

Radish Soup   22

BEETS

Cooking Methods   23

Orange-Infused Beet and Pasta Salad   24

Beet and Beaujolais Soup   25

CARROTS

Moroccan Carrots   26

Pickled Vegetables   27

Carrot Raita   28

EARLY VINES   29

PEAS

Risi Bisi Rice and Peas   29

Peas with Shrimp   30

Pasta with Peas, Ham and Cream   31

Pizza and Risotto for First Harvest 32

Pizza with Spinach, Prosciutto, Pine Nuts and Smoked Mozzarella Cheese 32

White Wine Risotto with Wilted Chard and Beet Greens 32

Crusty Pizza Dough and Basic Risotto 33

MID-SEASON HARVEST 34

ROOTS 35

POTATOES

Garlic Mashed Potatoes with Sautéed Cabbage 35

Potato Leek Soup 36

Roasted Potatoes with Rosemary 37

Potato Leek Frittata 37

Oven Roasted Vegetables 38

Potato and Fennel Salad 39

COLE CROPS 40

CAULIFLOWER

Spinach Noodles and Cauliflower with Mustard Butter 40

Cauliflower and Broccoli Salad 49

Turmeric Cauliflower 50

CABBAGE

Asian Stuffed Cabbage Leaves 51

Cabbage Salad with Peanut Dressing 52

BROCCOLI

Broccoli 53

Steamed Broccoli with Sweet and Hot Garlic Sauce 54

Curried Vegetables in Coconut Milk 55

ALLIUM FAMILY 56

ONIONS

A Soup of Many Onions 56

Sautéed Walla Walla Onions 57

Broiled Onion Slices 57

Onion Relish 58

Stuffed Peppers 59

GARLIC

Cooking Methods, Garlic Oil, Garlic Purée 60

Garlic Croutons 61

Skordalia 61

LEEKS

Leeks Glazed with Soy Sauce and Orange 62

Pizza and Risotto for Mid-Season Harvest 63

   Pizza with Roasted Potatoes, Caramelized Onion and Gorgonzola Cheese 63

   Risotto with Leeks and Peas 63

LATE HARVEST 64

LATE VINES 65

SQUASHES

Marinated Zucchini and Green Bean Salad 65

Summer Squash and Corn Pasta 66

Zucchini Gratin with Asiago Cheese and Thyme 67

Zucchini Stuffed with Chilies and Corn 68

Rasta Pasta 69

Ratatouille 70

CUCUMBER

Cucumber Salad with Scallops 71

Tsatziki 72

Cucumbers Sanbaizu 72

Cucumber and Lemon Soup 73

Cucumber Salsa 73

BEANS

Fagiolini all'Aglio 74

Sautéed Summer Beans with Cherry Tomatoes 74

Vegetable Garden Pasta 75

Summer Harvest Soup 76

TOMATOES 77

Oven Stewed Tomatoes 77

Panzanella Salad 78

Tomatoes with Goat Cheese 79

Greek Orzo Salad 80

CORN 81

Southwestern Corn Tart 81

Corn and Tomato Gratin with Basil 83

Fresh Corn and Shrimp Soup 84

Grilled Vegetables 85

Pizza and Risotto for Late Harvest 86

   Pizza with Fresh Tomato, Mozzarella and Basil 86

   Risotto with Green Beans, Tomatoes and Basil 86

Bibliography 87

About the Author, About the Photographer 88

A Brief History of Joe's Garden

JOE'S STORY

Joe Bertero was born in San Francisco, moved back to the old country with his parents and grew up near Genoa, Italy, where his family taught him about vegetable farming.

He returned to America during the First World War at the age of 17, eventually working on his uncle's truck farm here in Bellingham on Iowa Street. In those days there were a number of truck farms in the area. "Truck farms" were gardens that trucked their produce to grocery stores and neighborhood markets.

Joe married Ann Del-Tedesco in 1931, and, working side by side, they grew vegetables that were superior to their competition. Greengrocers would often label the vegetables "From Joe's" as a selling point.

In June 1933, Joe and Ann Bertero moved their farm from Iowa Street to the present location at 3100 Taylor Avenue. They retired in the 1980s, gradually turning over the farm to Carl and Karol Weston.

CARL'S STORY

Carl Weston began to work as a teenager for Joe Bertero at the garden on June 9, 1959 at 7:00 a.m.

Carl loves the real work of growing on the now 7.5 acres, and is proving to be a good steward to the land. Few other gardeners have the knowledge of contained space gardening that is so successful at Joe's.

All the weeding and harvesting is done by hand. No sprays have been used for over 16 years. Soil tests are regularly done and passed. By practicing sustainable agriculture, that is, by taking care of the earth responsibly, the garden will continue to thrive.

Carl tests experimental seed varieties for companies with the future in mind, and the future of the garden is secure. The Weston family believes that taste is more important than durability. Carl and Karol are passing the knowledge of gardening on to their son, Jason and his wife Wendy.

KAROL'S STORY

I was about seven years old when I saw Joe's Garden for the first time. The family was packed into a small Nash Rambler, driving along the streets of Happy Valley in Bellingham. We drove past the "hugest" garden I had ever seen. At home we had a kitchen garden which fed our family of nine, but this was something else. I looked at the rows of beans, carrots and lettuces. How could one family eat so many carrots? It was explained to me that the farmer grew produce for the stores in town.

What I never could have imagined at the age of seven was how much these gardens would affect the course of my life. Who would think that, at 18 years old and newly engaged, I would drive into Joe's with my sisters and see a young man, (not my fiancé) carrying a crate of lettuce on his shoulders, and that in that moment, everything would change? I said "bingo", slipped the engagement ring off my finger, and six month later, Carl and I were married.

In the years since, not much has changed. Joe's Garden still provides produce for the community. From my kitchen window I look down on the garden and watch the afternoon sun capture the fine water spray as it falls to earth. Each of the past 18 growing seasons has provided precious memories and friendships. Customers become good friends, former workers return to show their children where they worked happily in the summers, and people visit from all over the world.

The hours are long and the pace is fast—this is a rich and rewarding life. By mid-October, the long straight green rows of vegetables are plowed under forming dark rich furrows for the winter. This is the happiest moment in a farm woman's eye, when the garden is an earth tone color. The "Closed for Season" sign is hanging on the barn door. Vacation time has come and we will look forward to another season a few months from now.

Introduction

"If you are not up to a little magic occasionally, you shouldn't waste time trying to cook."

—COLETTE

Good cooking begins with good ingredients. This book showcases the exceptional produce from Joe's Garden, the little farm that is a jewel of rural life in an urban setting.

Visiting the garden, we return to a simpler time that appeals to all of our senses. Navigate the tricky parking lot. Enter the shed and the abundant display of seasonal, fresh vegetables evokes memories of another time. Harvested, rather than processed, these vegetables are the real thing.

Using vegetables as the soul of the dish, we can enjoy all the flavors of the garden. Bringing a side dish to the center of the plate we can recall the "old country" way with vegetables, creating humble and satisfying dishes.

The produce at Joe's, especially the carrots and peas, taste perfectly delicious eaten right out of the garden and especially good in your car on the way home.

Simplicity is the key when dealing with these outstanding vegetables and the recipes in this book are just that. Enjoy!

—*Mary Ellen Carter*

First Harvest

After a long winter, we enjoy the fresh taste of spring. The garden has been seeded in February for enjoyment in May. A delightful variety of edible greens is ready. They can be divided into two broad groups: the softer, more delicate greens, eaten uncooked, and the sturdier greens which usually require cooking. In the former category, the loosely-folded leaf lettuces lend a sweet taste and pretty color to a salad bowl while the pale-leafed iceberg and romaine lettuces add a satisfying crunch. Sturdy greens such as spinach and beet greens, picked early, can be used uncooked in a salad mix, but more often a quick braise is necessary. These greens are bold and full of flavor and include the ever-popular and versatile spinach, and chard, which has a meatier texture with a forthright, earthy flavor. ❋ The digging forks and wheelbarrows are brought out of the sheds as the harvesting of the root crops begins. The cool moist weather through the nights and the warm afternoons are ideal for their growth. ❋ Radishes are the very first to burst from the earth, followed by tender young beets and the good-natured carrots. ❋ The bushel baskets are pulled out of the attic, ready to be filled with freshly-picked shelling peas, the hallmark of spring at Joe's. These are all sure signs that we have survived the winter months and we now look forward to a productive season.

LEAFY GREENS

Spicy Romaine Lettuce with Avocado and Lime ✻

1 head romaine lettuce, washed and drained, torn into pieces

1 small Walla Walla onion, sliced

2 small zucchini squash, sliced 1/4 inch thick

16 cherry tomatoes, halved

1 red or yellow bell pepper, thinly sliced

1 jalapeno pepper (optional), seeded and diced

4 radishes, sliced

1 cucumber, sliced

1 avocado, sliced

Cilantro leaves for garnish

Bring a quart of water to a boil and add a little salt. Add the squash, boil just a few minutes. Drain. Place it in a bowl of cold water to stop the cooking. Set aside. Prepare all the vegetables. Prepare the vinaigrette. Pour the vinaigrette over the vegetables and gently mix. Place the romaine in the bottom of a salad bowl. Set the vegetables on top. Garnish with cilantro.

LIME VINAIGRETTE

Zest and juice of 2 limes

1 tablespoon rice vinegar

3 tablespoons cilantro, chopped

1/4 teaspoon cumin

1 clove garlic, minced

Salt to taste

6 tablespoons olive oil

Combine the first six ingredients in a small bowl and whisk in the oil.

Serves 6

Dilled Mushroom and Mixed Lettuce Salad ✻

1 head romaine lettuce, washed and drained, torn into pieces

1/2 pound mushrooms, thinly sliced

3 medium tomatoes, cut into wedges

1/4 cup toasted sunflower seeds

Fresh dill for garnish

Place the lettuce leaves in a salad bowl and add enough of the dressing to coat the leaves; mix. Reserve some of the dressing. Place the mushrooms and tomatoes on the lettuce and sprinkle with the sunflower seeds. Pour remaining dressing over the top and garnish with the dill sprigs.

DILL DRESSING

3/4 cup homemade, or your favorite mayonnaise

1/2 teaspoon Dijon mustard

2 tablespoons fresh lemon juice

1 tablespoon fresh dill, chopped

Salt and pepper

Add the mustard, lemon, dill, salt and pepper to the mayonnaise and mix.

Serves 6

Spinach with Sautéed Shallots and Goat Cheese ✳

3 tablespoons olive oil

2 large shallots, sliced

2 teaspoons grated zest from 1 large lemon

2 pounds spinach, washed and drained

2 ounces goat cheese, crumbled

Heat oil in a large skillet or wok over medium heat. Add the shallots and cook until golden, three to four minutes. Add lemon zest and spinach, and continue cooking until spinach is wilted but still bright green, about three to five minutes. Remove from heat, add salt and pepper to taste and toss with goat cheese.

Serves 4–6

JOE'S EQUIVALENTS

1 bunch (4) beets = 1 pound

4 medium yukon potatoes = 1 pound

1 bunch chard = 1 pound

1 bunch carrots = 1.5 pounds

1 cauliflower = 2.5 pounds

1 cabbage = 2.5 pounds

3 tomatoes = 1 pound

1 romaine lettuce = 2 pounds

Spinach Salad with Sesame Seeds ❈

1/4 cup soy sauce

2 teaspoons sugar

2 tablespoons canola oil

2 tablespoons sesame seeds

1 pound spinach, washed and drained

1 tablespoon sesame oil

Mix the soy sauce, sugar and canola oil in a small saucepan and heat until the sugar is dissolved. Toast the sesame seeds until they are browned and popping. Place the spinach in a large salad bowl and pour the sauce over the top. Sprinkle with the seeds, drizzle a little sesame oil over the spinach and toss.

Serves 6

Fennel, Orange and Spinach Salad ✵

1 handful almonds, blanched
1 fennel bulb
2 oranges
2 large bunches spinach, washed and drained
1 dozen black olives
1 tablespoon chopped fennel greens for garnish

Preheat the oven to 350 degrees. To blanch the almonds, bring a few cups of water to a boil, drop the almonds in, turn off the heat and let them sit for a few minutes. Pour the water off and peel. Slice the almonds in half lengthwise and place them in the oven to toast for 10–15 minutes. Cut the bottom off the fennel bulb and discard tough leaves, slice thinly. Cut the peeled oranges into rounds, top with one tablespoon of the vinaigrette. Dress the spinach with the remaining vinaigrette and toss with the oranges, fennel, almonds and olives.

ORANGE VINAIGRETTE

Juice and zest of one orange
1 shallot, minced
1 tablespoon rice vinegar
1 teaspoon balsamic vinegar
1/2 teaspoon salt
6 tablespoons olive oil

Combine the first five ingredients in a small bowl and whisk in the oil.

Serves 6

CHARD   *Both the lush, dark green leaves and the thick white ribs of the chard plant can be eaten, each cooked in different ways. The leaves are steamed, sautéed or stuffed. The stems are delicious stewed or grantinéed. It is best to separate the leaves from the ribs before cooking. Loosely fold the leaf in half along the stem, grasp the folded leaf in one hand and separate the stem by pulling it away from the leaf with the other hand.*

Linguine with Swiss Chard and Walnuts ✳

1 1/2 cups shelled walnuts, chopped

2 pounds Swiss chard, washed

4 tablespoons olive oil

5 shallots, minced

4 garlic cloves, minced

Salt and pepper

1 pound linguine, cooked according to package directions

1/4 pound Jack cheese, grated

Place walnuts in a large skillet and toast over medium heat for about ten minutes. Set aside. Trim the chard, discarding tough stems and coarsely chopping the leaves. Heat the oil in a large skillet over medium heat. Add the shallots and garlic and cook about ten minutes until soft. Add the chard and season with salt and pepper to taste. Cook until leaves have wilted. Meanwhile, cook the pasta and drain, reserving 1/4 cup of the cooking water. Add the pasta and liquid to the chard mixture. Stir in cheese and walnuts and serve.

Serves 6

Braised Swiss Chard ☀

2 pounds Swiss chard, washed
1/4 cup olive oil
2 garlic cloves, minced
3 anchovies, chopped
6 tomatoes, chopped
Freshly ground black pepper

Place the chard in a pot of boiling salted water and cook for ten minutes; drain and chop. Squeeze dry. In a large skillet, heat the oil with the garlic for one minute. Add the anchovies, stir in the tomatoes and cook for 25 minutes. Add the chard and season with salt and pepper to taste. Stir and cook for ten minutes.

Serves 4

Italian Rice and Chard Soup ☀

2 bunches red or green chard, washed
1/4 cup olive oil
1/4 cup onion, minced
3 cups chicken broth
1/4 cup Arborio rice
1/3 cup basil leaves, julienned
Grated Parmesan cheese

Remove the stems of the chard and cut them into 1/4-inch pieces. Set aside. Bring a large pot of salted water to a boil and blanch the chard leaves for less than one minute until limp. Transfer to a colander and drain. Heat the oil in a large pot and sauté the onion and chard stems three to five minutes. Add the chicken broth and rice and simmer for 15–20 minutes until rice is cooked. Add the chopped chard and heat. To serve, top with the grated cheese and basil.

Serves 6

Wild and Weedy Greens ✳

1 teaspoon fresh ginger, minced

2 cloves garlic, minced

2 scallions, chopped

1/4 teaspoon black pepper

2 tablespoons vegetable oil

2 bunches mixed greens—chard or spinach, washed and drained

Chop the greens into three-inch pieces. Sauté ginger, garlic, scallions and pepper in the hot oil for about one minute. Add greens and stir until wilted, about five minutes. Stir in the sauce and serve.

SAUCE

1–2 tablespoons soy sauce

1 tablespoon sesame oil

1 teaspoon Asian chili sauce

1 tablespoon oyster sauce

1 tablespoon vinegar

Combine the ingredients in a small bowl and whisk.

Serves 4

Sautéed Beet Greens with Garlic ❋

2 tablespoons extra virgin olive oil

2 cloves garlic, minced

4 slices Pancetta, cut into small pieces

2 bunches beet greens

1/4 teaspoon red pepper flakes

Salt and pepper

In a large skillet, heat the oil and sauté the garlic and Pancetta until crisp. Chop the greens roughly and add to the skillet. Cook until greens are limp, about five minutes. Season with salt and pepper to taste.

Serves 4

OLIVE OIL

Cold press extra virgin olive oil is the first press of the harvest. It has a dark green color and is well suited for salad dressings and when you want a forceful olive taste. After the first cold press, the olives are heated and pressed again creating a virgin oil. Subsequent heatings and pressings produce lighter-colored, milder, all-purpose olive oils.

ROOTS

RADISHES   *The very first of the roots to burst from the earth in spring. Often relegated to the salad bowl—this puréed soup is a lovely color and as fresh and natural as spring.*

Radish Soup ✳

2 bunches radishes, washed, tops removed, julienned
2 tablespoons raspberry vinegar
4 cups broth (chicken or vegetable)
3 cups potatoes, peeled and cubed
1/4 cup chives, chopped
Juice of one lemon
1/4 cup white wine
Salt and pepper
Chive blossoms for garnish

Reserve 1/2 cup of the radishes to add to the finished soup. Toss together remaining radishes and vinegar and set aside. In a medium pot, bring the broth and potatoes to a boil and simmer until potatoes are soft. Add the radish mixture and simmer for five minutes. Transfer to a food processor or blender and purée. Remove from the heat and add the reserved radishes, chives, lemon and vinegar. Season with salt and pepper to taste. Garnish with chive blossoms and serve.

Serves 4

BEETS   *Beets have an earthy flavor. They are a true standout in the garden and in the kitchen with their flamboyant jewel color. Fresh, young and tender beets need little preparation.*

Beets ❋

COOKING METHODS

OVEN ROAST   For best flavor and color, place washed beets in a baking pan. Cover tightly with foil and bake at 375 degrees for about one hour. The skins will slip right off.

MICRO-BRAISE   Cut beets into uniform pieces and place in a casserole dish. Add 1/4 cup water. Cover tightly with plastic wrap and microwave on high for eight to ten minutes. Season with salt and pepper and continue with recipe of choice.

HERB BUTTER

2 sticks butter at room temperature
2 cloves garlic, minced
2 tablespoons fresh lemon juice

2 cups parsley, minced
Salt and pepper to taste

In a mixing bowl combine the butter and lemon juice until creamy. Add the garlic and parsley and season with salt and pepper to taste. Shape into a log and chill. Slice a small pat to place on top of a salmon or halibut steak just before serving.

Orange–Infused Beet and Pasta Salad ✳

4 medium cooked beets (see page 23)
1 teaspoon orange zest
1/4 cup orange juice
1 shallot, minced
2 cloves garlic, minced
1 1/2 teaspoons rice vinegar
1/2 teaspoon sugar
1 tablespoon stone ground mustard
1/4 cup olive oil
1/2 pound penne pasta, cooked according to package directions
1/4 cup hazelnuts, chopped
Chopped chives for garnish

Cook the pasta and drain. Chop beets into bite-size pieces and toss with the pasta and orange zest. In a small saucepan bring the orange juice, shallots, vinegar, sugar and garlic to a boil, lower the heat and simmer for about two minutes until the liquid is syrupy. Stir in mustard. Drizzle in oil, while whisking. Pour the warm vinaigrette over the pasta and stir. Garnish with hazelnuts and chives.

Serves 4

Beet and Beaujolais Soup ❋

8 medium beets, peeled and cut into 1/2-inch pieces
1 small red onion, chopped
1 ripe medium pear, cut into 1/2-inch pieces
3 tablespoons raw white rice
4 1/2 cups water
1 tablespoon sugar
2 tablespoons raspberry vinegar
2 cups Beaujolais wine
Salt and pepper
2 teaspoons finely-grated lemon zest
Crème fraiche for garnish

Place the beets, onion, pear and rice in a soup pot. Add the water, bring to a boil and reduce heat to simmer, cooking until the beets are very tender, about 30 minutes. Stir in the sugar, vinegar and wine. Allow the soup to cool and purée in a blender or food processor. Season with salt and pepper to taste. Garnish with a dollop of crème fraiche and sprinkle with lemon zest.

Serves 8

CARROTS   *Among the most good-natured of vegetables, carrots are adaptable to an endless variety of preparations. They are essential in broths and stews, though Carl's carrots are best eaten straight from the garden.*

Moroccan Carrots ❋

1 pound carrots

1/4 cup olive oil

2 tablespoons balsamic vinegar

1 tablespoon red wine vinegar

1/2 teaspoon paprika

1/2 teaspoon cumin

2 cloves garlic, minced

1/2 cup fresh parsley, chopped

Salt to taste

Peel, trim and slice the carrots on the diagonal. Place in a large pot and add cold water to cover. Cook over high heat until carrots are tender, yet crisp, five to seven minutes. Drain immediately. Whisk the oil and the two vinegars in a bowl. Add the spices. Add the hot carrots to the dressing. Season with salt to taste. Sprinkle with parsley.

Serves 4

Pickled Vegetables ❋

6 carrots, sliced

12 radishes

2 pounds zucchini squash, sliced thin

1 onion, sliced 1/4 inch thick

4 celery stalks, sliced

2 tablespoons kosher salt

3 cups white vinegar

1 1/2 cups sugar

1 tablespoon celery seed

1 tablespoon fennel seed

2 tablespoons ground mustard

3 dried hot peppers

In a large bowl, combine the vegetables and salt. Cover with cold water and let sit for 45 minutes. Drain thoroughly. In a large pot combine the vinegar, sugar, celery seed, fennel seed, mustard and dried peppers. Bring to a simmer. Remove from the heat and pour mixture over vegetables. Allow to cool and refrigerate at least one day. Vegetables may be stored in the brine for up to one month in the refrigerator.

Serves 12

WHY KOSHER SALT?

Of all the familiar types of salt, kosher salt will dissolve much faster than table salt, adding a lovely crunch when sprinkled on vegetables with less iodine aftertaste and more flavor.

Carrot Raita ❋

3 carrots, peeled and grated

2 green chilies, seeded and chopped

1/2 teaspoon salt

1/2 teaspoon sugar

1 cup plain yogurt

1/3 cup peanuts, chopped

3 sprigs cilantro, chopped

In a food processor, grind the garlic, chilies, salt and sugar together. Add to the yogurt and stir until smooth. Pour over the carrots and mix. Sprinkle the peanuts and cilantro over the top and serve.

Serves 6

CHIMICHURRI

This is an Argentinian sauce that goes well with veggies, chicken or chops.

10 cloves garlic, peeled and minced

1/2 cup minced flat leaf parsley

2 teaspoons dried oregano

1 tablespoon pepper flakes

1 cup olive oil

1/4 cup red wine vinegar

Salt and pepper to taste

Mix in a small bowl and set aside for two hours for taste to develop. Refrigerate.

EARLY VINES

PEAS   *The hallmark of spring is the harvesting of Joe's famous peas. The varieties grown are shelling, snaps and snow. The best in the Northwest. Note: One pound of fresh peas in the shell is roughly equivalent to one cup of shelled peas. Peas should be eaten within hours of picking so the sugar will not turn to starch.*

Risi Bisi
Rice and Peas ❈

4 green onions, chopped
4 tablespoons butter
2 cups shelled peas
4 cups hot chicken broth
1 cup short grain rice
2 tablespoons parsley, minced
Salt to taste
1/2 cup freshly-grated Parmesan cheese

Sauté the onions gently in the butter in a deep saucepan with a lid. Add the peas and cook one to two minutes. Add the broth, rice and parsley. Bring to a boil, cover. Reduce heat to simmer and cook about 20 minutes until the rice is cooked. Season with salt to taste. Stir in the cheese.

Serves 4

Peas with Shrimp ❋

1/2 pound snow peas, trimmed

1 pound shrimp, shelled and deveined

1/4 cup vegetable oil

1 clove garlic, minced

1 tablespoon fresh ginger, minced

1 jalapeno pepper, seeded and minced

4 green onions, chopped

1/2 red bell pepper, slivered

2 tablespoons sesame oil

1 tablespoon rice wine vinegar

Heat the oil in a wok and add the garlic, ginger, jalapeno pepper and green onions. Cook for two minutes. Add the shrimp and stir constantly until they turn pink, about five minutes. Combine sesame oil and vinegar and pour over the shrimp and peas. Serve over rice.

Serves 4

Pasta with Peas, Ham and Cream ✳

2 pounds fresh peas, shelled

1/2 stick butter

Salt to taste

1/2 Walla Walla onion, chopped

1/4 pound ham, diced

1/2 cup heavy cream

Freshly ground black pepper

1/3 cup freshly-grated Parmesan cheese

1 pound penne pasta, cooked according to package directions

Place two tablespoons of the butter in a medium saucepan with the peas and 1/4 cup water and cook over medium-high heat for about ten minutes. Salt to taste. Heat the remaining two tablespoons of butter in a skillet and sauté the onion until limp. Add the ham and cook about five minutes. Swirl in the cream and add a liberal grinding of black pepper. Add the pasta and toss. Sprinkle with cheese.

Serves 4

PIZZA FOR FIRST HARVEST

Follow the recipe for Crusty Pizza Dough on the following page and top with this seasonal suggestion:

Pizza with Spinach, Prosciutto, Pine Nuts and Smoked Mozzarella Cheese ❋

Sauté one pound of spinach with four cloves of chopped garlic over medium heat until wilted. Brown the pine nuts until golden. Julienne about two ounces of prosciutto. Drain the spinach and garlic mixture, and spread over the pizza dough. Sprinkle with pine nuts and prociutto and top with 1/4 pound of grated smoked mozzarella cheese.

RISOTTO FOR FIRST HARVEST

Follow the recipe for Basic Risotto on the following page and try this seasonal variation:

White Wine Risotto with Wilted Chard and Beet Greens ❋

2–3 stalks chard leaves, stems removed, leaves chopped
Greens from 4 beets, chopped

Sauté the greens in a little butter and garlic until wilted. Substitute 1/2 cup of white wine for the broth. As you stir in your last cup of broth, add the greens. Garnish with chopped parsley.

Crusty Pizza Dough ❋

2 cups flour
1/2 teaspoon salt
1/2 teaspoon sugar
1 package quick-rise yeast
3/4 cup warm water
1 tablespoon olive oil
2 tablespoons cornmeal

Dissolve yeast in warm water in a large bowl. Let stand for five minutes. Add the salt, olive oil, one cup of flour and mix. Add more flour until the dough holds together. Turn the dough out onto a lightly floured surface and knead until smooth, about ten minutes. Place in an oiled bowl. Cover and let rise in a warm place, free from drafts, until doubled in size, about one hour. Punch dough down. Shape the dough into a round and place on a cooking sheet sprinkled with cornmeal. Top with seasonal vegetables. Bake at 450 degrees for 15–20 minutes. Makes one 14-inch pizza.

Basic Risotto ❋

1 large Walla Walla onion, finely chopped
1 tablespoon olive oil
4 tablespoons butter
1 1/3 cups Arborio rice
3–4 cups chicken broth
1/2 cup freshly-grated Asiago cheese
Freshly ground black pepper

Sauté the onion in the olive oil and 1/2 the butter for about five minutes until translucent. Add the rice and stir well for three minutes to coat the grains. Add about 1 1/2 cups of broth and stir until it is absorbed. Continue adding 1/2 cup of broth at a time until the rice has absorbed all the broth. If the rice is too chewy add a little more broth. This will take about 20–25 minutes. Remove from heat and stir in the cheese and remaining butter and serve.

Serves 4

Mid-Season Harvest

JUNE AND JULY

As the summer days warm, we cut leafy heads of cabbage and sturdy broccoli spears which are often referred to as "Italian asparagus" by the immigrants that brought them here in the 1930s. The snow white color of the cauliflower is caused by the large outer leaves turning inward, keeping the sun away. The "flower" cannot create chlorophyll and remains white. Harvesting these cole crops is a two-man operation—one person pushing the wheelbarrow between the rows, while the second person chooses "the cut", as the thinning process is called, and tosses the head into the barrow. ❄ This is the first appearance of the famous Walla Walla onions. These sweet onions grow to an immense size at Joe's and since they cannot be stored over the winter they are enjoyed in the spring and summer. The most common of vegetables taste wonderful. Two kinds of potatoes are dug—red and gold. ❄ Garlic is synonymous with Joe's Garden. One of nature's more power-ful seasonings, garlic is a member of the lily family. Folklore has credited the bulb with being a tonic, a stimulant, a cure for the common cold, an aid to digestion and with having the power to ward off vampires. ❄ Shallots grow in pairs. They have a distinctive character of their own, a more intense flavor with less heat and harshness than onions. An essential ingredient in sauces and vinaigrettes, they are used in recipes where an onion would overpower. ❄ Before the discovery of the potato, leeks were the mainstay for the winter months in Europe. Leeks would be left in the ground and harvested when needed. The most subtle of the allium family, they have a particularly delicate taste in the spring and summer.

POTATOES *It has been said that you can make anything from a potato. Suitable for salads, soups, gratins and stews, this South American vegetable is rich in starch, minerals, protein and high in vitamin C and potassium.*

Garlic Mashed Potatoes with Sautéed Cabbage ❈

1 pound Yukon gold potatoes, peeled and quartered
4–6 cloves whole garlic
2 cups chicken broth
1 cup water
1/2 cup milk
1/2 pound cabbage, finely shredded
2 green onions, finely chopped
Salt and pepper
Finely-chopped fresh parsley for garnish

Place potatoes and garlic in a saucepan and cover with the broth and water. Bring to a boil and cook for 20 minutes or until tender. While the potatoes are boiling, melt two tablespoons of butter in a skillet. Add the cabbage and stir until wilted. Add the green onions and set aside. Drain the potatoes and add milk, salt and pepper and beat at medium speed with a mixer until light and fluffy. Stir in the cabbage and onion. Sprinkle with parsley.

Serves 4–6

Potato Leek Soup ✤

6 leeks (1 1/2 pounds)
4 tablespoons butter
5 medium potatoes, peeled and cut into chunks
3 cups water
3 cups chicken broth
1 cup milk
Salt and pepper
Chopped chives for garnish

Cut off the tough, dark green top portion of the leeks leaving about three inches of the light green stalk and rinse. Slice in half and then chop into one-inch pieces. Heat the butter in a soup pot over low heat until foaming, stir in leeks and cook until tender, about ten minutes. Increase heat to high and add the water, broth and potatoes. Bring to a boil, then lower heat and simmer until the potatoes are tender, about 20 minutes. Let cool slightly and purée in a food processor or blender. Add the milk and chill. Season with salt and pepper to taste. Add more milk if you prefer a thin soup. Garnish with chopped chives and serve chilled.

Serves 4

Roasted Potatoes with Rosemary ✳

2 pounds small red potatoes
2 tablespoons olive oil
8 cloves garlic, unpeeled
4 sprigs fresh rosemary
Salt to taste

Preheat oven to 400 degrees. Scrub the potatoes and remove any damaged areas. Heat the oil in an ovenproof skillet. Add the potatoes and mix well to coat them with oil. Add the garlic, rosemary and salt. Bake for 30 minutes, then turn the potatoes over and bake 30 minutes longer. Gently press the garlic with a fork and squeeze it out of its skin over the top of the potatoes. Serve immediately.

Serves 4–6

Potato Leek Frittata ✳

2 tablespoons olive oil
1 large leek, rinsed and sliced into thin rounds, tops discarded
2 red potatoes, boiled and sliced into rounds
2 sprigs fresh parsley, chopped
1/3 cup grated Jack cheese
Salt and pepper
6 large eggs, beaten

Preheat oven to 350 degrees. Heat the oil in a large ovenproof skillet. Sauté the leeks until soft, about five to ten minutes. Add the potatoes and parsley and stir. Beat the eggs in a bowl, stir in the cheese and season with salt and pepper to taste. Pour mixture into skillet and cook until the bottom of the eggs are set, about five minutes. Transfer skillet to the oven and bake until the top is set or firm to the touch, about five to seven minutes. Serve at room temperature.

Serves 4

Oven Roasted Vegetables ✳

1/3 cup olive oil

8 small new potatoes, cut in half

1/2 Walla Walla onion, chopped

8 baby carrots

8 red radishes

3 chard stems, cut into 3-inch pieces

2 large garlic cloves, peeled

1 sprig thyme, chopped

1 bay leaf

Juice of 1–2 lemons

1/2 cup black olives

Salt

1/2 bunch basil, julienned

Grated Romano cheese

Preheat the oven to 400 degrees. Toss the prepared vegetables in a bowl with the olive oil, thyme, bay leaf and a little salt. Spread the vegetables in a single layer in a roasting pan. Roast in the upper third of the oven, about 25–30 minutes or until tender. Remove from the oven and squeeze the lemon juice over the vegetables. Add the olives and mix. Serve with the basil garnish and a sprinkling of Romano cheese.

Serves 4

BASIL OIL

This is a cold infusion of basil and olive oil. Drizzle over fresh tomatoes or pasta.

1 cup very fresh basil leaves   2 cups extra virgin olive oil

Sterilize a pint canning jar. Wash and dry the basil leaves (I use a salad spinner). While the jar is still hot, pack it with leaves. Pour the olive oil over the leaves and cover. Let sit in a cool dark place for ten days. Keep in the refrigerator.

Potato and Fennel Salad ✻

1 pound small potatoes, scrubbed
1 fennel bulb
12 cherry tomatoes
1/4 pound feta cheese
1/2 onion, minced
4 sprigs basil, chopped

Cook the potatoes in water until tender, about 15 minutes. Clean the fennel bulb and remove tough outer ribs. Slice thinly. Toss the onion and fennel in the vinaigrette. Season with salt and pepper to taste. Cut the warm potatoes into slices and add. Toss gently. Crumble the feta cheese over the top and garnish with tomatoes and basil.

VINAIGRETTE

1/4 cup rice wine vinegar
1/3 cup olive oil
1/4 cup water
1 tablespoon Dijon mustard
Salt and pepper

Mix the vinaigrette ingredients in a large salad bowl until blended.

Serves 4

COLE CROPS

CAULIFLOWER   *Mark Twain said "Training is everything. Cauliflower is nothing but cabbage with a college education."*

Spinach Noodles and Cauliflower with Mustard Butter ✳

6 tablespoons soft butter

2 tablespoons Dijon mustard

3 shallots, finely diced

2 cloves garlic, minced

2 tablespoons vinegar

2 tablespoons parsley, roughly chopped

3–4 cups broccoli and cauliflower florets

1 pound spinach fettuccine, cooked according to package directions

Salt and pepper

1 cup bread crumbs

Grated Parmesan cheese

Cream four tablespoons of the butter with the mustard, shallots, garlic, vinegar and parsley. Set aside. Melt the remaining butter in a skillet, add the bread crumbs and cook until crisp. Set aside. Bring a large pot of water to a boil and drop in the broccoli and cauliflower. Cook for about one minute. Melt the mustard butter over a low flame. Scoop the vegetables out with a slotted spoon and add them to the melted mustard butter. Bring the vegetable water back to a boil and cook the pasta. Toss with the vegetables. Season with salt and pepper to taste. Sprinkle with the bread crumbs and a little cheese.

Serves 4

Cauliflower and Broccoli Salad ✳

1 head cauliflower, broken into florets
1 bunch broccoli, broken into florets

Steam the broccoli and cauliflower for about six to eight minutes until fork tender. Allow to cool. Toss in a salad bowl with the dressing, garnish with red pepper slices and serve.

DRESSING

4 cloves garlic
1 egg
1 tablespoon Dijon mustard
3/4 cup olive oil
1 tablespoon white wine vinegar
1 teaspoon kosher salt
Juice of 1/2 lemon
1/8 teaspoon white pepper
Red bell pepper slices for garnish

Purée the garlic cloves in a food processor or blender. Add the egg and the mustard. While the machine is running, add the oil slowly until it has thickened. Season with the lemon juice, vinegar, salt and pepper.

Serves 6

Turmeric is part of the ginger family, similar in shape to ginger but a little smaller. Slice the skin off and you will see bright orange flesh. When it is dried it loses all its moisture, thus concentrating the color. Turmeric is a spice that generally turns everything it touches sun gold, except when a pinch is added to a green vegetable, then it intensifies the green and holds it.

Turmeric Cauliflower ✳

1 whole cauliflower, broken into florets
1 tablespoon canola oil
1/2 teaspoon turmeric
1/4 teaspoon ground red pepper
1 cup chicken broth
1 1/2 teaspoon salt
1 handful cilantro, chopped

Heat the oil in a large skillet over medium heat. Add the turmeric and cook until it is aromatic. Add the cauliflower, toss, and add salt, pepper and broth. Cover and simmer for ten minutes until tender. Uncover and continue cooking until the moisture evaporates, about five minutes. Sprinkle with cilantro and serve.

Serves 4–6

Asian Stuffed Cabbage Leaves ❋

8 large cabbage leaves
1 tablespoon vegetable oil
Salt and pepper
1 tablespoon fresh lemon juice
3 chopped green onions for garnish

Plunge the cabbage leaves into boiling water and blanch for one minute. Lay out the leaves. Divide the stuffing among the leaves, leaving the edges clear. Turn in the sides of each leaf, roll like a cigar and tie with kitchen string. Heat the remaining tablespoon of oil in a saucepan or wok that is large enough to hold the leaves in a single layer. Gently turn the leaves in the oil. Add water to cover the leaves halfway. Add the lemon juice, salt and pepper to taste. Cover and simmer ten minutes. Carefully remove the stuffed leaves to a platter, garnish and serve.

STUFFING

1 tablespoon vegetable oil
1 red bell pepper, chopped
1 carrot, shredded
1 cup cooked rice
1 inch fresh ginger root, grated
1 teaspoon rice vinegar

Heat the oil in a wok over medium heat. Add the pepper, carrots, cooked rice and ginger. Stir well. Sprinkle with vinegar.

Serves 4

Cabbage Salad with Peanut Dressing ✳

1 medium cabbage, chopped

2 carrots, julienned

1 cucumber, julienned

1 handful bean sprouts

1 handful basil or mint

4 green onions, chopped

Prepare the dressing and let stand for 30 minutes. Prepare the vegetables and place in a large salad bowl. Pour the dressing over the top of the vegetables and mix.

DRESSING

2 cloves garlic, minced

1 inch fresh ginger root, grated

1/4 teaspoon red pepper flakes

1/4 cup smooth peanut butter

1/4 cup soy sauce

2 tablespoons oyster sauce

1/2 cup vegetable or chicken broth

Whisk the ingredients in a small bowl until well blended.

Serves 8

This following recipe is a tasty way to cook broccoli—it stays bright green in color, and has a slight crunch.

Broccoli ✳

1 bunch broccoli, separated into stalks
1 cup water
1 tablespoon olive oil
3 cloves garlic, minced
Salt and pepper

Peel the broccoli stalks and cut into two-inch pieces. Bring the water to a boil in a large saucepan. Add the broccoli, cover and cook three to four minutes. Drain. Heat the oil in a large skillet. Add the garlic and toss in the broccoli. Season with salt and pepper to taste. Serve immediately.

Serves 4–6

GREMOLATA

Sprinkle this Italian garnish over steamed vegetables to add a little "punch".

Zest of 2 lemons   5 tablespoons fresh basil, chopped
2 cloves garlic, minced   4 sprigs parsley, minced

Combine the ingredients in a small bowl and mix.

Steamed Broccoli with Sweet and Hot Garlic Sauce ✳

2 bunches broccoli, broken into florets

Put an inch of water in the bottom of a steamer and bring to a boil. Place trimmed and peeled broccoli pieces with stems about 1/2 inch thick in a steamer basket and cook about five to seven minutes. Coat with sauce and serve.

SAUCE

1 cup sugar
1/2 cup water
1/2 cup vinegar
2 tablespoons garlic, minced
1 teaspoon salt
1 tablespoon chili garlic sauce (found in the Asian section of the market)

In a medium saucepan combine sugar, water, vinegar, garlic and salt. Bring to a boil, stirring until sugar dissolves. Reduce the heat and simmer until syrupy, about 20 minutes. Remove from heat and stir in the chili garlic sauce. Let cool, transfer to a jar, cover and refrigerate. The sauce will keep up to three weeks.

Serves 6

Curried Vegetables in Coconut Milk ❈

3 tablespoons vegetable oil

1 onion, chopped

3 cloves garlic, minced

2 stalks broccoli, broken into florets

3 carrots, sliced into rounds

1 red pepper, sliced lengthwise

1 yam, peeled and cut into 1-inch cubes

1/2 head cauliflower, broken into florets

1 14-ounce can coconut milk

2 tablespoons yellow curry paste

1/3 cup orange juice

1/2 pound spinach, cleaned

1/2 cup cilantro, chopped

Heat the oil in a wok or large skillet, add the onions and garlic and cook for two minutes. Add the cauliflower, broccoli, carrots, pepper and yam to the wok and cook for ten minutes. Mix the curry paste with the coconut milk and add to the wok. Cover and simmer for 15 minutes. Add the spinach, cilantro and orange juice and cook for five minutes. Garnish with cilantro. Serve over Jasmine rice.

Serves 6

ALLIUM FAMILY

A Soup of Many Onions ※

4 small new potatoes, scrubbed and quartered

6 cups chicken broth

2 tablespoons butter

1 Walla Walla onion, peeled and sliced

3 leeks, trimmed and sliced

4 green onions, peeled and sliced

3 cloves garlic, peeled and sliced

1 cup milk or half and half

Salt and pepper

Chopped chives for garnish

Put the potatoes and broth in a large pot and bring to a boil over medium-high heat. Reduce heat and simmer for about 10–15 minutes until the potatoes are tender. Drain and reserve broth. Meanwhile, melt the butter in a large skillet and add the Walla Walla onions, green onions, leeks and garlic. Cook until soft, about 15 minutes. Add the potatoes and cook for a few minutes more, then remove from the heat. Purée the soup in a blender, then return to the pot and thin with the milk or half and half. Season with salt and pepper to taste and garnish with the chives.

Serves 6

Sautéed Walla Walla Onions ※

4 medium Walla Walla onions, sliced
4 tablespoons butter
2–3 tablespoons balsamic vinegar
Salt and pepper
Several branches fresh thyme, chopped

Melt the butter in a sauté pan or skillet. When it foams, add the onions, and sauté over high heat for four to five minutes. They will be lightly browned, sweet and still a little crunchy. If you prefer them softer, continue to cook, then add the vinegar. Stir quickly as the vinegar cooks away. Season with salt and pepper to taste and thyme leaves.

Serves 4–6

Broiled Onion Slices ※

1 pound Walla Walla onions
1/4 cup melted butter or olive oil
Salt and pepper
1 pound Gruyère cheese

Slice onions 1/2 inch thick. Place on the rack of a broiling pan, brush with butter or olive oil and season with salt and pepper. Broil until they turn a delicate brown color. Turn with a spatula and brush again with butter. Season with salt and pepper. Heap shredded Gruyère cheese on the top and return to the oven just long enough to melt the cheese.

Serves 4

Onion Relish ✳

1 Walla Walla onion, chopped

1/2 cup stuffed green olives with pimientos, drained

1/4 cup extra virgin olive oil

1/2 handful fresh basil, chopped

2 tablespoons capers, drained

1 tablespoon red wine vinegar

1 sprig fresh oregano, chopped

Combine ingredients in a food processor and pulse until mixed. Let stand at room temperature for at least one hour. Makes two cups.

The marmalade balances the sweetness of the sugar with the sourness of the vinegar, citron and the piquant green tomatoes.

Green Tomato Marmalade ✳

2 pounds green tomatoes, chopped

1 orange, sliced thin, seeds removed

1 lemon, sliced thin, seeds removed

1 1/2 cups sugar

4 tablespoons balsamic or red wine vinegar

2 inches fresh ginger root, finely chopped

1/2 teaspoon salt

Pinch cayenne pepper

Put tomatoes, orange and lemon in a shallow pot with sugar, vinegar and seasonings. Boil uncovered for 20–30 minutes or until liquid is thick and syrupy. Mixture will thicken as it cools. Makes two cups.

Stuffed Peppers ✳

3 meaty red or yellow bell peppers (or any combination), halved and seeded
3 tablespoons olive oil
1 onion, chopped
1 cup steamed long grain rice
1 cup grated cheddar cheese
2 tomatoes, coarsely chopped
2 tablespoons minced parsley
1/2 teaspoon salt
1/4 teaspoon pepper
1 cup bread crumbs

Preheat the oven to 350 degrees. Oil a shallow baking dish. Cook the peppers in boiling water for two to four minutes, drain and set aside. Heat the oil in a skillet and sauté the onion until soft. Mix the onions, rice, cheese, tomatoes, parsley, salt and pepper. Fill each pepper half with the mixture and sprinkle the tops with the bread crumbs. Bake 35–40 minutes until lightly browned.

Serves 4–6

VARIATIONS

Substitute one pound of ground beef or lamb for the rice and cheese. Add the meat to the skillet after the onion is soft and cook until browned. Mix with the rice, tomatoes, onions and spices. Continue to follow the recipe above.

If you like anchovies add about 1/2 can of anchovy fillets to the onion. Add three cloves of garlic, two tablespoons lemon juice and some black olives. Mix with rice, tomatoes and spices. Continue to follow the recipe above.

Garlic ❄

COOKING METHODS

SAUTÉ   Heat a little olive oil in a pan and cook chopped garlic until lightly browned which will develop a nutty garlic flavor.

OVEN ROAST   Combine the cloves with a little olive oil, salt and pepper. Place on a square of aluminum foil, fold and crimp the edges to seal. Roast on a cookie sheet at 400 degrees for about 30 minutes.

BAKE   Preheat the oven to 375 degrees. Lightly oil the entire bulb and sprinkle with salt and pepper. Place the bulbs in a shallow roasting pan and bake for about 45 minutes until the garlic is soft. To eat the garlic, squeeze interior out with the flat side of a knife and spread on toasted French bread.

GARLIC OIL

Finely chop two cloves of garlic and cover generously with olive oil. Store garlic oil in the refrigerator and use it to sauté or season other dishes.

GARLIC PURÉE

1 dozen heads garlic
2–3 tablespoons olive oil
Salt

Separate the heads into cloves, leave the cloves in their papery husks and simmer in a pan of water seasoned with one teaspoon salt for 35 minutes, or until soft. Drain, then put through a food mill to extract the soft pulp. Season the purée with a touch of salt and mix in two tablespoons of oil. Put in a jar. Cover the top with one tablespoon of oil to create a thin film. Can be stored in the refrigerator for two weeks.

Note: Always store peeled and chopped raw garlic in the refrigerator.

Garlic Croutons ✳

2 tablespoons olive oil
2 garlic cloves, finely chopped
1/4 loaf rustic bread, thinly sliced
Freshly-grated Parmesan cheese

Preheat oven to 375 degrees. Combine olive oil and garlic. Lay the slices of bread on a baking sheet and brush lightly with the garlic oil. Bake for about five minutes until bread is crisp and golden brown. Sprinkle with Parmesan cheese.

A delicious Greek dip—serve with crunchy vegetables and pita wedges.

Skordalia ✳

5 pieces French bread, crusts removed
3 big garlic cloves
1 medium potato, peeled and boiled
1/4 teaspoon salt
1/4 cup olive oil
3 tablespoons fresh lemon juice

Wet the bread with water and squeeze out the moisture. Place in a food processor with the garlic and process until well blended. Add the potato and salt and process again. While the motor is running, pour in the oil in a slow, steady stream and then add the lemon juice. Can be refrigerated for ten days. Makes two cups.

LEEKS   *The bottom of the leek is grown underground. Sand often gets inside the leaves so they require careful washing. To prepare leeks for cooking, cut off the green part and trim the roots. Cut them in half lengthwise and wash under running water spreading the leaves apart.*

Leeks Glazed with Soy Sauce and Orange ✳

3 tablespoons soy sauce
2 tablespoons fresh orange juice
1 1/2 teaspoons rice vinegar
1 1/2 tablespoons honey
8 slender leeks or 2 per person

Prepare coals for grilling or preheat the broiler. Combine the soy sauce, orange juice, vinegar and honey in a saucepan and stir over medium heat until the honey is dissolved and the glaze thickens, about three minutes. Brush the leeks all over with this mixture and grill until tender, about 12 minutes, turning the leeks halfway through the cooking time.

Serves 4

PIZZA FOR MID-SEASON HARVEST

Follow the recipe for Crusty Pizza Dough on page 33 and top with this seasonal suggestion:

Pizza with Roasted Potatoes, Caramelized Onion and Gorgonzola Cheese ❊

Thinly slice 1/2 pound new potatoes, toss with olive oil and roast at 350 degrees for five to six minutes until tender and a little crisp. Over low heat sauté two sliced Walla Walla onions in a little olive oil and/or butter for about 30 minutes. Top with potatoes and onions. Dot the pizza with 1/4 pound of Gorgonzola cheese and sprinkle with snipped rosemary.

RISOTTO FOR MID-SEASON HARVEST

Follow the recipe for Basic Risotto on page 33 and try this seasonal variation:

Risotto with Leeks and Peas ❊

Remove the tops of three or four leeks and sauté in two tablespoons butter or olive oil over medium heat until soft. Season with salt and pepper to taste. During the final ten minutes of cooking the risotto add 1/2 pound fresh green peas and the leeks and garnish with a handful of chopped parsley.

Late Harvest

This is the busy time for us. We put in long hours. The picking schedule starts with corn in the cool temperature of the morning. This vegetable is greeted with much ritual and celebration. ❋ The beans are picked after the dew is gone. Romano beans are the flat stout Italian variety and are grown only at Joe's Garden. They are about six to eight inches long and are a hearty, flavorful type. The more familiar Blue Lake snap beans and a French variety of string bean, "haricot vert" are also available, picked at their peak of snap and sweetness. ❋ Tomatoes are picked in the noonday sun. When the vine-ripened tomato crop is at it's bright red peak, chefs know it's hard to improve on their flavor and serve them simply seasoned with salt, pepper and a sprinkling of fresh basil. Nature provides this perfect combination of sun-drenched tastes for us to enjoy. Joe's tomatoes are sold with the stem still attached and the unmistakable aroma of being vine ripened. ❋ Crisp and juicy cucumbers are harvested along with the tender summer squash, including green and gold zucchini, when they are about six inches long. ❋ Summer squash's light unassertive flavor makes it one of the most versatile of vegetables, lending it to a wide variety of preparations. ❋ The much-anticipated garlic harvest is very satisfying. This is a heavy job. A daily task, it requires weeks of digging, washing, drying, rolling and braiding. While Joe braids, he chooses only the best garlic for next year's seed stock. ❋ The season is in full swing!

LATE VINES

Marinated Zucchini and Green Bean Salad ✺

1 pound zucchini squash, sliced into 1/2-inch rounds
1/2 pound green beans, trimmed and sliced
6 mushrooms, sliced
3 green onions, chopped
1 sprig fresh dill, chopped
1/3 cup rice wine vinegar
1/3 cup olive oil
Salt and pepper

Blanch the zucchini and green beans by submerging them in boiling water for three to five minutes. Place in a salad bowl and add mushrooms and green onions. Mix the dill, oil and vinegar. Season with salt and pepper to taste. Pour over vegetables and refrigerate one hour.

Serves 4

Summer Squash and Corn Pasta ✳

4–6 small summer squash, diced

6 ears corn, kernels cut from the cob

2 cloves garlic, minced

1 jalapeno pepper, diced

3 tablespoons olive oil

Salt and pepper

1 handful cilantro leaves

2 tablespoons butter

4 tablespoons water

1 pound fettuccine, cooked according to package directions

Juice of 1/2 lemon

Sauté the squash in the olive oil until tender. Season with salt and pepper. Add the corn, garlic and jalapeno to the squash and continue to cook a few minutes more. Finely chop the cilantro and set some aside for garnish. Add the cilantro, butter and water to the pan. Season with salt and pepper to taste. Add the cooked fettuccine and toss. Squeeze the lemon over the top. Garnish with the reserved cilantro.

Serves 4

Zucchini Gratin with Asiago Cheese and Thyme ❋

2 tablespoons olive oil

1 large Walla Walla onion, chopped

1 1/2 pounds ripe tomatoes, sliced

1 1/2 pounds zucchini squash, cut into 1/4-inch slices

3 tablespoons olive oil

1/4 cup fresh thyme sprigs

1 teaspoon kosher salt

1 1/2 cups grated Asiago cheese

Freshly-ground black pepper

Heat the olive oil in a medium skillet over medium heat. Add the onion and sauté until golden brown. Preheat the oven to 375 degrees. Toss the squash slices in a medium bowl with 1 1/2 tablespoons of the olive oil, two tablespoons thyme, and 1/2 teaspoon salt. Sprinkle one tablespoon of thyme over the onions in the bottom of a large baking pan. Starting at one end, lay a row of slightly overlapping tomato slices across the width of the pan and sprinkle with a little cheese. Next, lay a row of squash overlapping the tomatoes by 2/3 and sprinkle with cheese. Repeat the rows until the pan is full. Season lightly with pepper and the remaining salt. Drizzle with the remaining olive oil and sprinkle with thyme and then a final topping of cheese. Cook until well browned and until the juices have bubbled, about 60–70 minutes. Let cool for at least 15 minutes before serving.

Serves 6

Zucchini Stuffed with Chilies and Corn ✴

1/2 teaspoon olive oil

2 cloves garlic, minced

1 small onion, chopped

2 ears corn, kernels cut from the cob

1 can hominy, drained

2 large eggs

2 chilies, seeded and minced

Salt and pepper to taste

2 large zucchini squash, cut in half lengthwise

4 teaspoons Monterey Jack cheese

1 green onion, chopped

Preheat the oven to 375 degrees. Heat the oil in a saucepan over medium heat. Sauté the garlic and onion until soft, about five minutes. Let cool. Purée half the hominy and half the corn in a food processor, add the eggs and mix. Transfer to a bowl and stir in the onion, remaining corn and hominy, chilies, salt and pepper. Scoop the seeds out of the zucchini and fill them with the corn mixture. Place in a shallow baking dish and pour in one cup of water. Cover with foil and bake for 30 minutes. Uncover and continue baking until tender, about another 30 minutes. Sprinkle with the cheese, return to the oven and bake until melted. Serve garnished with chopped green onion.

Serves 4

Rasta Pasta ✳

THE VEGETABLES

2 tablespoons olive oil

1 green pepper, sliced

4–6 mushrooms

2 small zucchini squash

1 bunch broccoli, broken into florets

Juice of 1/2 lemon or lime

1 pound pasta, cooked according to package directions.

In a large skillet, heat the oil and sauté the pepper, mushrooms, zucchini and broccoli for five minutes. Squeeze the lemon or lime into the pan and simmer. Add the cooked pasta. Coat with sauce and serve.

THE SAUCE

2 tablespoons olive oil

1 small onion, diced

2 cloves garlic, minced

1 inch fresh ginger root, grated

2–3 chili peppers, minced

1 large yam, diced

1 cup chicken broth

2 cups coconut milk

1 teaspoon ground coriander

1 teaspoon cumin

1 tablespoon thyme leaves

1/2 teaspoon white pepper

1/2 teaspoon ground allspice

1/2 teaspoon salt

Heat the olive oil over medium heat and add the onion, garlic, ginger and chili pepper. Sauté five minutes. Add the yam and broth and cook for 15–20 minutes. Add the coconut milk, coriander, cumin, thyme, white pepper, allspice and salt and simmer for five minutes. Process in a blender until sauce is smooth.

Serves 6

Ratatouille ❋

2 tablespoons olive oil

1 medium onion, thickly sliced

Salt and pepper

6 cloves garlic, finely chopped

4 Japanese eggplants, cut in half lengthwise, sliced 3/4" thick

2 bell peppers, cut into thick slices

1 pound summer squash, cut into thick slices

2 pounds tomatoes, chopped

1 bay leaf

1 teaspoon fresh oregano

1/2 cup fresh basil, chopped

Heat the olive oil in a large skillet and add the onion, 1/2 teaspoon salt and a few pinches of pepper. Sauté over medium heat until soft. Add the garlic, eggplant and peppers and cook for about ten minutes or until the peppers are just tender. Add the summer squash, tomatoes and bay leaf and cook over low heat for 20 minutes. Add the basil and oregano just before serving. Season with salt and pepper to taste.

Serves 4

Cucumber Salad with Scallops ✳

4 medium cucumbers, peeled, seeded and cut in half lengthwise

Salt

2 tablespoons fish sauce

Juice of 2 limes

1 clove garlic, finely minced

1 small chili or 1/4 teaspoon red pepper flakes

1 tablespoon lemon grass, minced

1/2 teaspoon sugar

6 cups mixed salad greens

1 1/2 pounds sea scallops

1 tablespoon canola oil

1/2 teaspoon salt

1/8 teaspoon cayenne

1/2 cup each chopped mint and cilantro

2 teaspoons sesame oil

Sprinkle the cucumbers with salt and let them drain for about 30 minutes. Rinse lightly and cut into 1/4-inch slices and place in a bowl. Mix together the fish sauce, lime juice, garlic, chili, lemon grass and sugar. Thin with a tablespoon of water. Toss with cucumbers and set aside. Place the scallops in a bowl and toss with the canola oil, salt and cayenne. Heat a skillet over high heat and add the scallops. Do not crowd them. Cook for about two minutes per side, until just done. Place salad greens on a large platter. Toss the cucumbers with half the mint and cilantro and pour over the greens. Top with the scallops. Drizzle with the sesame oil and sprinkle with the remaining mint and cilantro.

Serves 4

Tsatziki ✳

2 cups plain yogurt

2 cucumbers, peeled, seeded and chopped

2 cloves garlic, minced

1 tablespoon vinegar

2 tablespoons olive oil

Salt and pepper

Drain the cucumber in a sieve or colander. Add the garlic, vinegar, olive oil, salt and pepper to the cucumbers and mix. Add yogurt and blend. Makes 2 1/2 cups.

Cucumbers Sanbaizu ✳

2 cucumbers, peeled and seeded

Cut the cucumbers into paper thin slices. Pour about half the Sanbaizu sauce over the cucumbers and drain. Pour the remaining sauce over the cucumbers and serve at room temperature.

SANBAIZU SAUCE

1 cup rice vinegar

1 cup Dashi (available in Asian markets)

4 tablespoons soy sauce

2 tablespoons sugar

In a medium-size saucepan bring all ingredients to a simmer, stir and cool.

Serves 4

Cucumber and Lemon Soup ☀

4 cucumbers, peeled, seeded and coarsely chopped
Juice of 2 lemons
1 teaspoon kosher salt
1 tablespoon honey
1 cup yogurt
1 cup water
1 large tomato, chopped
Fresh dill sprigs
Sour cream

Place cucumbers, lemon juice, salt, honey, yogurt and water in a blender and purée until very smooth. Pour mixture into a large bowl, cover and refrigerate overnight. Purée the tomato and add to the soup before serving. Season with salt and pepper to taste. Serve in chilled bowls with a garnish of dill and a dollop of sour cream.

Serves 4

Cucumber Salsa ☀

2 cucumbers, peeled and chopped
2 cloves garlic, minced
2 green onions, chopped
1–2 Thai chilies, minced
1/4 cup fresh lime juice
1/4 cup cilantro, chopped
1/4 cup mint, chopped
1/4 cup fresh basil, julienned
1 1/2 teaspoons kosher salt
1 teaspoon sugar
1/2 teaspoon freshly-ground black pepper

Combine all the ingredients. Let stand for one hour before serving. Store in the refrigerator. Makes two cups.

Fagiolini all'Aglio ✳

3 tablespoons olive oil

1 pound Romano beans, stems and tips removed

Salt and pepper

2 cloves garlic, chopped

1/2 cup freshly-grated Asiago cheese

Heat the olive oil in a sauté pan. Add the beans, lightly salt and pepper and cook for about ten minutes until they lose their crunch. Mix in the garlic for the last two minutes of cooking. Sprinkle with cheese and serve immediately.

Serves 4

Sautéed Summer Beans with Cherry Tomatoes ✳

1 pound Romano beans, trimmed and cut into 1-inch pieces

1 tablespoon olive oil

1 shallot, diced

1 clove garlic, minced

1 1/2 teaspoons fresh lemon juice

2 tablespoons dry white wine

Salt and pepper

1/2 pint cherry tomatoes, cut in half

1 tablespoon fresh tarragon or basil

Bring a large pot of water to a boil, plunge in the beans and cook until bright green and tender, about four minutes. Drain. Heat the oil in a sauté pan, add the shallots, garlic, one teaspoon of the lemon juice and the white wine. Add the beans and salt and pepper and sauté about two to three minutes. Add the cherry tomatoes and herbs and cook just until the tomatoes are cooked through without losing their shape. Season with salt, pepper and the remaining lemon juice.

Serves 4

Vegetable Garden Pasta ✳

1 red bell pepper, cored, seeded and sliced

1 green bell pepper, cored, seeded and sliced

1 sweet onion, thinly sliced

4 cloves garlic, minced

3 small zucchini squash, sliced

2 small crookneck squash, sliced

1 handful green beans, snapped

8 small carrots, julienned

2 large ripe tomatoes, chopped

Several sprigs basil, chopped

1/2 cup olive oil

Salt and pepper

1 cup chicken broth

Juice of 1/2 lemon

2 tablespoons butter

1 pound fettuccine

Fresh parsley for garnish

Sauté the onions in 1/4 cup of the olive oil until translucent. Add half the garlic, the peppers, salt and pepper and cook for four minutes. Add the squash, tomatoes, basil and chicken broth and cook over a high flame for about three minutes. Add the remaining oil, garlic and a squeeze of lemon. Remove from the heat and stir in the butter to enrich the sauce. Bring water to a boil in a large pot and add the pasta. About three to four minutes before the pasta is done add the carrots and beans. Drain. Place the fettuccini in a warm bowl and pour the vegetables over the top. Garnish with parsley.

Serves 4–6

Summer Harvest Soup ❋

1/4 cup olive oil

2 medium onions, chopped

3–4 chard stems, chopped

2 quarts chicken or vegetable broth

4 new potatoes, diced

2 large tomatoes, coarsely chopped

1/2 teaspoon fresh thyme

1 medium zucchini squash, diced

1 crookneck squash, diced

2 ears corn, kernels cut from the cob

1/4 pound Romano beans, cut into 1-inch lengths

1/2 cup orzo pasta

1/2 cup chopped parsley

1/2 cup cilantro pesto, below

Heat the oil and cook the onion, garlic and chard stems until golden. Add the broth and bring to a boil. Add the potatoes, tomatoes and salt to taste. Bring to a simmer for 30 minutes. Add the squash, corn and beans and simmer for five minutes. Add pasta and simmer until al denté, about ten minutes. Stir in parsley and pesto. Serve with additional pesto.

Serves 8

CILANTRO PESTO

2 bunches cilantro, stems removed

6 cloves garlic

1 cup Asiago cheese, grated

2 tablespoons fresh lemon juice

Blend the cilantro, garlic and cheese together in a food processor until finely chopped. Add the lemon juice to make a paste. Makes about 2/3 cup.

TOMATOES

Oven Stewed Tomatoes ✳

4 large ripe tomatoes

1 14.5-ounce can peeled plum tomatoes

4 cloves garlic, minced

3 tablespoons olive oil

1 branch fresh thyme

12 red cherry tomatoes

12 yellow cherry tomatoes

1 handful fresh basil leaves

Preheat the oven to 375 degrees. Blanch the tomatoes in boiling water for one minute and peel. Arrange the fresh and the canned tomatoes, along with their juice in a large baking dish. Sprinkle the garlic over the tomatoes. Drizzle with the oil and lay the thyme branch on top. Season with salt and pepper. Bake for 30 minutes. Add the cherry tomatoes and heat until they just burst, about 10–15 minutes. Place in a serving bowl and garnish with basil leaves.

Serves 4–6

Panzanella Salad ✻

1 loaf Italian peasant bread, cut into 1-inch cubes
1/2 Walla Walla onion, chopped
1 fennel bulb, trimmed and chopped
1 cucumber, peeled and chopped
3 large tomatoes, chopped
1 handful Italian flat parsley, chopped
1 handful basil leaves, chopped
Fennel leaves for garnish

Toss the salad ingredients with the vinaigrette, garnish with fennel leaves and serve immediately.

VINAIGRETTE

3 tablespoons red wine or Balsamic vinegar
1/2 teaspoon kosher salt
1/2 cup extra virgin olive oil
Freshly-ground black pepper

Combine the vinegar and salt in a small bowl and slowly whisk in the oil. Add freshly-ground pepper to taste.

Serves 4–6

Tomatoes with Goat Cheese ❋

1 pound tomatoes
1/2 pint cherry tomatoes
1 bunch watercress
Salt and pepper
2 ounces mild goat cheese

Core the tomatoes and cut into wedges. Leave the cherry tomatoes whole or cut in half if large. After washing the watercress, spread it on a serving platter and arrange the tomatoes on the top. Lightly salt and pepper the tomatoes and drizzle with the vinaigrette. Crumble the goat cheese over the top.

VINAIGRETTE

3 tablespoons red wine or Balsamic vinegar
1/2 teaspoon kosher salt
1/2 cup extra virgin olive oil
Freshly-ground black pepper

Combine the vinegar and salt in a small bowl and whisk in the oil. Add freshly-ground pepper to taste.

Serves 4

TRADITIONAL SALSA

4 tomatoes, diced
3 green onions, chopped
2 cloves garlic, minced
1/2 bunch cilantro, chopped

1 jalapeno or more, seeded and
   chopped
Juice of 1/2 lime
Salt and pepper to taste

Combine all ingredients in a bowl and mix well. Makes two cups.

Greek Orzo Salad ☀

1 cup orzo pasta

6 tablespoons olive oil

5 tablespoons red wine vinegar

1 small red onion, minced

2 cloves garlic, minced

1 1/2 teaspoons salt

1/2 teaspoon pepper

1 teaspoon dried oregano

1/4 cup parsley, minced

2 large tomatoes, chopped

1 cucumber, peeled and chopped

16 Greek olives

6 ounces feta cheese

Bring two quarts of water to a boil, add the pasta and cook about eight to ten minutes. Drain and toss with one tablespoon of the olive oil. In a bowl, whisk the oil, vinegar, onion, garlic, salt, pepper, oregano and parsley together. Pour over the pasta while still warm. Add the tomatoes and cucumbers to the pasta and sprinkle with the olives and feta cheese.

Serves 6

CORN

Southwestern Corn Tart ❋

1 tablespoon olive oil

1/2 small red onion

2 ears corn, kernels cut from the cob

Cayenne pepper

2 jalapeno peppers

2 tablespoons cilantro, chopped

1 tablespoon fresh oregano

3 eggs

1 1/2 cups half and half

1/2 cup grated white cheddar cheese

Salt

Tart dough (see page 82)

Preheat oven to 375 degrees. Prepare the tart dough. Heat the olive oil in a large sauté pan, add the onion and cook about three to five minutes until soft. Add the corn, 1/8 teaspoon of cayenne pepper and a little salt and sauté another five minutes. Remove from heat and toss with the jalapenos and herbs. Allow to cool. Beat the eggs in a medium bowl, add the half and half, a pinch of salt and cayenne to taste. Spread the cheese on the bottom of the tart dough, top with the corn and onion. Pour the custard over the filling and bake for 35–40 minutes, until the custard is set. Makes one 9-inch tart.

Serves 4–6

TART DOUGH

1 teaspoon dry yeast
Pinch of sugar
1/4 cup warm water
1 cup white flour
1/2 teaspoon salt
1 large egg
3 tablespoons unsalted butter at room temperature
Flour for shaping

Dissolve the yeast and sugar in the water and set in a warm place. Combine one cup flour and salt in a bowl. Break the egg into the flour and add the butter and yeast. Mix to form a smooth dough. Set aside in a warm place and allow to double in size, about 45 minutes. Use a nine-inch tart pan with a removable bottom. Flatten the dough, place it in the center of the pan and press into an even layer. Use only enough flour to keep from sticking. Once the tart is filled, bake at 375 degrees for 35–45 minutes.

Corn and Tomato Gratin with Basil ✳

2 tablespoons olive oil

1 1/2 cups onion, chopped

7 ears corn, kernels cut from the cob

Pinch of nutmeg

Cooking spray

2 1/2 cups half and half

3 large eggs

2 large egg whites

1/4 teaspoon hot pepper sauce

2 cups tomatoes, diced

1/2 cup basil, chopped

Preheat oven to 350 degrees. Heat olive oil in a large skillet over medium heat and sauté onions until soft, about four minutes. Add corn kernels and continue cooking for another five minutes. Add the nutmeg and season with salt and pepper to taste. Set aside. Coat a two-quart casserole with cooking spray. Combine the eggs, half and half, egg whites and hot sauce in a large bowl and whisk. Stir in the corn mixture. Pour into casserole and bake until set, about 30 minutes. Top the casserole with the diced tomatoes seasoned with salt and pepper and return to the oven, cooking until they are heated, about ten minutes. Sprinkle with basil and serve.

Serves 6

Fresh Corn and Shrimp Soup ✳

1 teaspoon butter or olive oil

1/2 onion, diced

3 cloves garlic, chopped

5 cups vegetable broth, homemade or canned

6 ears corn, kernels cut from the cob

1 ear corn, cut into 1-inch chunks

3/4 pound tomatillos, chopped

3 jalapeno peppers, seeded and chopped

1/2 pound shrimp, peeled and deveined

Salt and pepper

Cilantro pesto (see page 76)

Melt butter in a soup pot and sauté the onion and garlic until the onions are translucent. Set aside about two cups of the corn. Add the remaining corn kernels and a little salt to the onions. Stir in two cups of broth and simmer for 25 minutes. Add the tomatillos, jalapeno and chunks of corn along with the remaining broth and cook an additional five to ten minutes, until the tomatillos are tender. Purée the reserved corn in a blender or food processor with about one cup of broth until smooth, then add it back into the soup. Add the shrimp and cook until it turns opaque. Top with one tablespoon cilantro pesto and serve.

Serves 6

The secret to great grilled vegetables is keeping them from drying out. The basting sauce keeps the vegetables moist and delicious. Make sure the vegetables are cut into uniform pieces small enough to cook through properly and to pick up the smoky flavors in a short time.

Grilled Vegetables ❈

2 ears corn, each cut into 4 pieces
1 small eggplant, cut into 1/2-inch pieces
1 large red onion, cut into 3/4-inch pieces
2 large bell peppers, red or green, cut lengthwise into strips
2 large zucchini squash, quartered lengthwise
Salt and pepper
Lemon slices and sprigs of thyme for garnish

Arrange vegetable pieces in a single layer on a baking sheet and baste lightly with the sauce, reserving about 1/2 cup for dipping when serving. Prepare barbecue for medium heat. Grill the vegetables until they are tender and lightly charred, about six minutes. Brush occasionally with the sauce. Serve at room temperature with the dipping sauce on the side.

BASTING SAUCE

1 stick butter
1 shallot, minced
1/4 cup olive oil
3 tablespoons Dijon mustard
2 tablespoons fresh lemon juice
2 tablespoons thyme, chopped
1 tablespoon lemon zest

Combine all ingredients in a saucepan. Whisk over medium heat until melted and blended.

Serves 4

PIZZA FOR LATE HARVEST

Follow the recipe for Crusty Pizza Dough on page 33 and top with this seasonal suggestion:

Pizza with Fresh Tomato, Mozzarella and Basil ❋

Seed and slice four medium tomatoes. Place on top of the dough and spread with two cloves of finely-minced garlic. Sprinkle with salt and pepper. Top with 1/3 pound shredded mozzarella cheese and 1/2 cup grated Parmesan cheese. Before serving garnish with julienned basil leaves.

RISOTTO FOR LATE HARVEST

Follow the recipe for Basic Risotto on page 33 and try this seasonal variation:

Risotto with Green Beans, Tomatoes and Basil ❋

Blanch 1/4 pound green beans for two to four minutes. Chop and seed 1/2 pound of tomatoes. As you add the last cup of broth to the risotto, add the beans and tomatoes. Garnish with julienned basil leaves.

Bibliography

Sincere thanks to the following authors for their inspiration and adaptations:

Bettoya, Jo and Anna Maria Cronetto, *Italian Cooking In The Grand Tradition,* The Dial Press 1982

Brown, Edward Espe and Deborah Madison, *The Greens Cookbook,* Bantam Books, 1987

Chase, Sarah Leah, *Nantucket Open House Cookbook,* Workman Publishing Company, 1987

Cunningham, Marion, *The Fannie Farmer Cookbook,* 1979 Alfred A. Knopf, Inc.

Hazan, Marcella, *Marcella Cucina,* HarperCollins Publishers, Inc. 1997

Meyers, Perla, *Fresh From The Garden,* Random House 1996

Olney, Richard, *Lulu's Provençal Table,* HarperCollins Publishers 1994

Pepin, Jacques, *Jacques Pepin's Simple and Healthy Cooking,* Rodale Books, 1994

Somerville, Annie, *Fields of Greens,* Bantam Books 1993

Spear, Ruth, *The Classic Vegetable Cookbook,* Harper and Row 1985

Waters Alice, *Chez Panisse Vegetables,* HarperCollins 1996

About the Author

Mary Ellen Carter is a local food columnist and cooking instructor. During the past five years she has taught for the Whatcom County's Cultural Arts Program at the Roeder Home and is now teaching at the Whatcom Community College. She has published a cookbook on her Asian cooking class series, as well as a cookbook that highlights seasonal delights from her weekly column written for the Bellingham Herald. She lives with her husband Terry the "Taste Tester".

About the Photographer

Diane Padys brings over 20 years experience to achieve mastery in blending artistry with technical excellence in her photographs. This award winning photographer's expertise is attributed to rich professional experiences in New York, San Francisco and Europe. Diane's photo studio is in Seattle and she resides in Bellingham.